Living Then & Now

By

Richard A. Bowen

Published in the United States of America by
Ariadne Publishers, Brookfield, WI, U.S.A.
Phone: 414-444-2012
© Richard A. Bowen 2024. All rights reserved.
ISBN: 979320906188

Living Then & Now

Contents

Introduction i

Toys 4

The Neighborhood Environs 7

A Lightning Strike and Other Adventures 13

Boats, Forts, and Fire 15

Moving On.. 17

Other Boyhood Friends 20

Girls 23

Bands... 26

Pranks and Protests 30

Protest... 32

After High School 37

Wrap-Up.. 86

Introduction

This book is an implied comparison. I tell of my experiences, feelings, deeds, and thoughts with the intent to show what I went through while living my life that led up to a successful business career. At various stages I was new, experienced, confused, confident, open, closed, a failure, and a success. Anyone who has had the opportunity to operate their own business can relate, I'm sure.

I hope you enjoy this journey. Many stories, people, and much learning has helped me become a better person.

Living Then & Now

My earliest remembrances are from my parent's first house in Wauwatosa, Wisconsin, a suburb of Milwaukee. I was three years old playing outside on the sidewalk of the tree-lined street with a little boy named Corky. Why someone would name a child Corky perplexed me, then and now.

Corky and I rode our tricycles together, not straying far from the immediate area in front of the house, which was a two story American mid-century modern home that had a rec room in the basement furnished in 1950's style decorations and furniture – pink and black. Across the street lived our neighbors the Renelee's. They had a daughter named Vicki, my age, whom I was supposed to befriend, but I did not feel compelled to do that.

My parents had one car, a shiny maroon, Dodge four-door model that when I rode in it, hanging out one of the passenger side windows, I marveled at the "swoosh" as we drove passed other vehicles on the street. The car was massive inside, like many automobiles at that time, with a bubble top.

A few blocks up the street was a neighborhood park where my grandfather, when he visited, fed salted-in-the-shell peanuts to the squirrels, who occupied the park and lived in the tall elm trees that lined the neighborhood streets. One time, curiously because we lived far from a river or stream, we had a flood and the brown, ankle-high water, rushed down the middle of the street.

Living Then & Now

This was a German-influenced section of town and many homes were constructed of the local Lannon stone, a white, hard limestone that was mined from two quarries in the immediate area. Most of the houses were older brick edifices that looked like castles with turrets and gables, and were of heavy stone construction.

After playing with Corky on the tricycles for a year or so, I found out my family was moving. Our new house would be three miles west of the present house. It was a "tri-level" and bigger, with four bedrooms and three bathrooms, a large dining room and living room, den, and kitchen. My maternal grandfather gave my parents money to help build the new home, with the stipulation that he would live there until he passed away.

The builder and designer of the home was a man named Firsch who designed and built two similar homes in the area. (One can recognize Firsch-built homes because they have a distinctive chimney that slants at a 45-degree angle on one side, and the master bedroom is always located above the garage.)

My parents took us children, me, my older sister by two years, and my brother who was just a baby to see the new home as it was being built. At that stage in its construction, the house was only a series of two-by-fours over a cinder-block basement in a dirt-filled lot devoid of trees, plants, and shrubs.

Living Then & Now

After we moved in, I shared a top-floor bedroom with my brother. At first we slept in the same full-sized bed. A year later, my parents bought us twin beds. As a six-year-old kid, I remember telling them, "I want a headboard that has a shelf or storage area on it." I had seen a friend's bed and wanted one like it. They bought the beds that way, with matching dressers for each of us. The window coverings were beige curtains with color pictures of railroad engines on them.

My brother and I often played on the carpeting between the twin beds where there was enough room for two small boys and their toys. The beds and the space between as a play area was like a valley between two mountains. Adjacent to the play area was a dormer that jutted out into space from the house. Inserted in the inside of the dormer was a built-in bookcase, where we kept our kids' books. Some of them were the Christmas or birthday gifts we received, children's books that held only vague interest for us, with subjects such as the planets and science. But others that held a strange fascination were from my mother's childhood collection, books like the "Bunny Brown and His Sister Sue" series, *Grimm's Fairy Tales*, and the original *Wizard of Oz* by Frank Baumn. Later we got some books like *Space Travel*, *Curious George*, and a variety of Golden Books that included the Chip 'n Dale books, two adventurous chipmunks who rode on their own miniature train; Snow White; Cinderella; Pinocchio;

Alice in Wonderland; and others. (A few years later when my parents sold the piano bench where we stored our Golden Books, the books mistakenly went with the bench. We were heartbroken; we never saw the books again.)

Our bedroom, and the adjacent smaller bedroom across the hall where my sister slept, were located on the third floor of the house, the same floor as the attic, which meant it was hot in summer. We'd throw open the windows wide in the summer months in an attempt to coax a breeze into the rooms. It wasn't until a few years later that my parents bought an electric fan, which they placed in the hallway between the two rooms in order to circulate some air. By contrast, the attic in winter was extremely cold.

Toys

One of my friends had a safe where he stored the items he wanted to keep secret from everyone in his family. For my birthday I persuaded my parents to get me a safe, but compared to my friend's, mine was a toy. Although my safe was primarily metal, the door was clear plastic through which you could see the gears of the combination lock. It was not very secure, but I kept my "egg rock" in there, a stone I found that was shaped like an egg, and my coin collection, blue colored books full of pennies, dimes, nickels, and quarters that grew heavier with

Living Then & Now

every coin I added to the cardboard pages. All the dimes, quarters, and half-dollar coins were made of real silver. Some of the more interesting coins I collected were the steel pennies of the World War II era (not made of copper to help the war effort) and Indian head pennies.

Space travel was on everyone's mind at the time. One Christmas, Santa Claus brought me a rocket launcher. It had four different kinds of plastic rockets: the Thor, Redstone, Jupiter, and Atlas. You inserted one of the rockets onto the launch pad and set the timer, which stimulated a count down. When the timer hit zero, the launcher launched the rocket via a spring about a foot into the air – not terribly exciting but entertaining, nonetheless.

Long before Hotwheels, the toy that turned out to provide the most hours of fun was a miniature racetrack set. My friend had an Aroura brand set that ran on AC (alternating current). Those cars, about the size of Hotwheels, were cute but they literally vibrated down the track and emitted an irritating buzzing noise. Mine was an Atlas brand set that ran on DC (direct current). The cars ran smoothly down the track, their little electric motors humming quietly. We played with my racetrack set constantly, setting up the track in the original figure-eight pattern but then later configured it in a large oval and eventually a straight-way, like drag racetrack. We bought additional track and more

Living Then & Now

cars, while we modified the old ones with different bodies and bigger tires. Some of the prized cars we added to the set were Buick Rivieras and hotrods.

Before the racetrack set, I had gotten a Lionel train, which also provided hours of fun. One of the few things my dad built for me was a train table. (Dad usually did not build or make things for us kids because he felt it was better if we attempted to make what we needed ourselves, even if we failed. Something as big and complicated as a train table was the exception.) The table enabled me to avoid playing with the train set on the floor in the basement of the house.

My Lionel train was an old-fashioned steam engine made of heavy cast iron. The train had a coal car, a boxcar, a gondola car, a log-carrying car, and a caboose. When the train passed over a special track, it tripped the crossing guard, which was a little gate that went down and, mimicking real life, prevented automobiles from going on the track as the train passed by. When I put some smoke-liquid in the engine's smokestack, it merrily puffed white smoke. When I pushed a button on the transformer that ran the setup, the engine made a whistle sound from a by-gone era.

Bikes were big. For a while, I had a black and white 26-inch Schwinn three-speed called "The Racer" with a black saddle bag on the back. Then Schwinn came out with ten-speed models; other makers such

Living Then & Now

as Huffy came out with ten-speeds, too, but Schwinn was top of the line. Some friends in the neighborhood had gotten ten-speeds; I had to have one, too, a metallic blue one. One day Dad took me to the local bike shop, traded the three-speed for the blue ten speed, and my life was complete.

The Neighborhood Environs

Our house was located half-way up a hill overlooking a parkway, which is actually a county park that runs for miles north and south along the Menomonee River in that part of the state. Our street was called Park Ridge Avenue. In winter we would speed down the hill on our sleds on the snow and ice. The sleds had metal frames and runners, and wooden slats to lie or sit on. You'd steer by moving the metal frame from side to side, at least that was the theory. In reality, once you started going, you only had about a 50-50 chance of steering the sled at all.

For a real thrill, we would keep going past the end of the hill onto the relatively busy parkway. If a car would have been coming down the parkway, there's no way we could have stopped after careening down the hill, and we probably would have been injured or killed. But no one ever got hurt – not many cars traveled the parkway on snowy days. Taking the chance was part of the adventure.

Living Then & Now

My friend Adrian had an unusual toy, tailor-made for the neighborhood, where most of streets were on hills similar to ours. It was a sled like a snow sled but this contrivance had wheels instead of runners. One steered it like one steered a conventional sled: by moving the metal frame from side to side. We often rode this wheeled conveyance down our hill where we got going very fast; it seemed even faster as one lay on the frame with the asphalt whizzing by two inches below. One time, I lost control of the wheeled sled and slid on my face along the asphalt. That injury took a couple of weeks to heal.

In addition to sledding, the hill provided us with other kinds of entertainment. When it rained, the water formed gullies on the edges of the asphalt. We had loads of fun trying to dam up or otherwise divert the rushing water. The gravel that we found on the hill gave us building materials for the dams and walls we built for our plastic army men. The gravel felt moist and heavy in our hands as we constructed the edifices of our dreams.

Two of our neighbors had built large sandboxes for their kids. We played in them constantly and for hours, bringing our toy trucks and cars with us so we could have vehicles with which to traverse the roads and tunnels between the castles and sand houses we built from the wet sand.

The neighborhood had several vacant lots where grasses grew as tall as us boys. These natural areas

Living Then & Now

harbored marvelous insects and birds, and together with the wildflowers, plants, and grasses, gave each vacant lot its own personality. The two adjoining lots directly down the hill from our house had uneven ground and three granite boulders twice as tall as we were. The boulders were hard and cold to the touch as we patted them like old friends and wondered how they got there. The two lots were fenced off by a picket fence from the house that bordered them on one side.

On the other side was an incline and nearby were some old tin basins and a smokestack or chimney, long discarded and rusting and which filled with water when it rained. The boulders, the rusted tin stuff, and the uneven ground provided hours of entertainment and fun for all the kids in the neighborhood. We climbed the big rocks and played "king of the mountain," we made a witches' brew from the water in the tin basin, and we examined the flowers, plants, and insects as we lay in the grass between the little rolling hills.

The vacant lots up from our house on either side of the street were flat. The one on our side of the road was adjacent to a house that had a long-abandoned and empty swimming pool on the edge of the property. The red-painted concrete pool was a continuous focal point of fascination for us. We would go to the side of the old pool, look down into it, and wonder what it was like to swim in it when it was in use. This field also had an ancient pine tree with many branches that we could climb.

The field directly across the street from the one with the pine tree was the flattest one, which we made into a baseball diamond by borrowing a lawn mower and mowing the grass to make the paths between the bases. We played softball almost every summer evening until we couldn't see the ball anymore.

The fields in the neighborhood were our playgrounds but the real adventures took place in the Menomonee River parkway. Along our side of the river ran a path that paralleled the water. The story was that it used to be a bridle path for horses that belonged to a family who once lived in a fieldstone house two miles downriver. The house, guest house, and fences were still there but the horses were not. The path was kept open by people walking on it and especially by kids' bikes, and the dirt on the path was always packed down as a result. A big boulder which we called "counsel rock" lay in the middle of the path at one point. We imagined First Nation people meeting at the rock after walking up from the river which was easily accessible there. North of counsel rock was a group of old willow tree stumps that the river current had hollowed out. When the river was low, we could play inside the stumps, so we called them "tree houses."

Living Then & Now

A mile from our immediate neighborhood were the lagoons, two ponds that harbored ducks and turtles and on whose banks were large willow trees. These willows were so big that where the large bottom branches branched off to form the higher elevations of the tree they formed natural "platforms" that one could stand on. The trees were big enough to have many of these platforms, so when we played house in these trees, we named the adjacent platforms the "bedroom" or the "kitchen" or "the living room." We imagined these trees afforded us everything we needed to live there: shelter, enough room, and water from the lagoons.

Of course both the river and the lagoons froze in winter, not just for a few days but for the entire season. It was shoulder-to-shoulder people skating on the frozen lagoons, especially on the weekends. The county put up a warming house on the bank of one of the lagoons where a coal-burning stove kept the inside warm for the skaters. Skating from one lagoon to the other seemed like a mile away and sometimes the temperature was so low that skating there left you dangerously cold, so when you returned you were eager to follow the path of other skaters, climb onto the bank, and walk on your skates without losing your balance into the warming house.

The river itself could be treacherous for skating because the water was moving underneath the ice

Living Then & Now

and because sometimes, even in the coldest weather when the sun came out, it melted the ice in the middle of the river and especially in the rapids. But this made it challenging and no one that I knew ever fell in.

Skating on the river ice was surprisingly smooth, and it was adventurous because we could travel for miles, north or south, where we could discover new vistas. Mostly it was woods on either side of the river, up and down, but it was especially wooded on the west side of the river, which was undeveloped compared to "our" side of the river.

Our side was near to houses but also picnic tables and outdoor grills; the west side was just woods and flood plain, and in our minds, undiscovered country. We would explore the "other side" only once in a while when we were feeling extra adventurous in the warmer months. We had to make special effort to walk the half mile and cross the river over the highway bridge that led to that area. But it was worth it. The woods were untamed, giving us great opportunities to view wildlife, big trees, and plants that we would not normally see. Unfortunately, the only animals we usually saw were ducks. Canada geese had been hunted to near extinction and there were no whitetail deer at that time in the area. (Since that time, Canada geese have made an amazing recovery, and one often sees them and whitetail deer in the area today.)

Living Then & Now

A Lightning Strike and Other Adventures

One hot, humid summer night when the thunderstorms were active, we heard a loud crack in the middle of the night. The next morning, word spread through the neighborhood that the house two doors down from ours had been struck by lightning. Our parents inquired and the owners of the house granted permission to see the strike. We ventured up to a second-story bedroom. There we observed a hole about six inches in diameter where the lightning bolt had struck and where it had travelled all the way down to the basement.

Lightening entertained us often. We'd sit on my neighbor's metal swing set (probably not the wisest viewing choice during thunder and lightning storms) and watch the "lightning show."

The neighborhood continued to fascinate as we grew up. Next to Christmas, the big event of the year was Halloween. Even as small children, we dressed in a costume (usually a cheap ghost, devil, or angel dime-store one) and ventured out on October 31, after dark. There was no day- time trick-or-treating, nor did our parents accompany us. As boys, even thinking about our parents coming with us was unheard of and certainly would have eliminated the fun and adventure. Sometimes it was cold and we'd have to have wear our coats or jackets underneath our costumes. We'd knock on

Living Then & Now

the doors of every house in our immediate neighborhood and after we depleted that area of treats, we'd go farther afield to different and more remote areas, sections that we normally would not frequent. This was also part of the adventure because, especially at night, these neighborhoods seemed strange and foreboding. We visited people's homes whom we did not know and sometimes the occupants would invite us inside to check us out and ask us our names and where we lived.

We shied away from groups of kids we did not know for fear they might rob us of our booty. If our bags were too heavy with candy, we'd head home, drop them off, and get another one to keep going. The candy lasted for months. This, of course, was after we had carved our pumpkins and lit them with candles that were large enough to keep the pumpkins lighted for the many hours we were out trick-or-treating.

In summer we played games after dinner. These included "Kick the Can" and "Spud." When we played "Red Light, Green Light," we spread out through the neighborhood as we called out in sing-song voices, "Red light, green light, hope to see a ghost tonight!" We played baseball, rode our bikes, and explored until it was too dark to see anything anymore and we could hear our parents' voices calling us to come home. As we drifted homeward, the neighborhood became quiet and the stars came out. Only one streetlight lit up a small area of the road where our hill ended and the parkway began. Otherwise it was dark enough to see the planets, the stars, and occasionally the Aurora Borealis, waves of pale pink and green light undulating through the dark sky north of our house.

Boats, Forts, and Fire

My friend Eddie lived a couple of houses away from me. His father was an engineer and built Eddie a sailboat that had a real canvas sail and a rudder made from an old golf club. When I asked my father to build me a boat, he said, "Build one yourself," which I did. I cut a block of wood at an angle on each side to make the bow of the boat and put a stick in the middle for a mast. It was ugly but it floated in the water. I learned two things: I could make something if I tried and I was going to be going it alone; Dad was not going to do things for me.

Eddie's parents liked boats. They had two of them: a mahogany Chris Craft inboard-outboard motorboat that they kept on a trailer in their driveway for use on inland lakes, and a cabin cruiser that they kept in a slip in the harbor in Sturgeon Bay, Wisconsin, a community located on Green Bay about three hours north of where we lived. Eddie took me with them a few times when

Living Then & Now

their family vacationed there. We slept on the cabin cruiser and played on the water during the day.

Eddie's parents had bought him a dingy with a small, gasoline-powered outboard motor on it. He showed me how to get free gas. At one of the waterfront gas pumps where boats refueled, we took off the hose and placed the nozzle in the gas can that we had brought along. As Eddie explained, "There's always some gas left over in the hose." We raised the hose high in the air. Some leftover gas poured into our gas can. We did this a few times at other pumps and soon we had enough for our water excursions on his dingy for the day. These excursions consisted mainly of tooling about the Sturgeon Bay harbor, which was home to some major shipyards where they built big ships for the Navy. We'd take the dingy in front of the huge ships and peer up the bow, which was probably five or six stories above us. On Sunday, Eddie's mom would go to church in Sturgeon Bay. His dad, a non-believer, would stay home on the boat.

In the winter, Eddie and I would build snow forts that were big enough for two boys. One of the forts had a plywood roof. We built a fire inside of it, and it got smoky in there. We also made forts in summertime out of various pieces of wood we found around the neighborhood.

We were always looking to do something with fire; it held a compelling fascination. In warmer weather, we'd often take our bikes to the parkway and find a secluded spot to build a campfire so we could roast our hotdogs. Or we would build rafts out of wood and start them on fire before sailing them down the river, not realizing the fire hazard we were creating.

Moving On

As I grew older, I began to expand my friends and my horizons. I knew Scott from the second grade at school. I attempted to befriend him but he obviously was not interested, But I kept trying. One time I grew so frustrated that I burned a photograph of him and gave the ashes to him in a glass bottle. Maybe that turned the corner because a few weeks later, he agreed to come over to my house on a Saturday afternoon. His mother dropped him off in her white 1959 Mercury hardtop, and picked him up afterwards. (Later, as adults, Scott told me he did not want to hang out after school like I had asked him to because he wanted to go home and watch "Leave it to Beaver" on television.)

Next, it was my turn to visit Scott's house. After my parents dropped me off, Scott showed me his room. It had tons of model ships and cars. Then we toured his walk-out basement where he was growing beans and potatoes hydroponically. I was in awe. This guy was a scientist. He also showed me his candy-red, professional drum set. Next we set out for a walk down by the Menomonee River, which ran near his parent's property. Scott explained that they made "forts" out of the reeds that grew profusely along the riverbanks and also made spears from the same reeds. He said, "We recently had a war with the kids from Butler (a town upriver from his house) and fended off their attack." Now I was doubly in awe.

Bruce lived up the street from Scott and we sometimes hung out after school. He invited me over to watch TV and eat Walgreens ice cream, which his parents kept liberal amounts of stored in their freezer.

Of course, the big influence at this age was school. Webster Grade School was located very much in Scott's and Bruce's neighborhood. It was far away from my home; we had to walk almost two miles to get there, which we did, unaccompanied and with no complaints. The school was a large edifice with two floors, and a lunchroom, kitchen, and a classroom in the basement. The district added two wings for kindergarten classes later. The building had two baseball diamonds on the asphalt portion of the playground and another one on the grassy area. The school also had another large field across the street which the school flooded in the winter to create an ice rink and which the student athletes used for track and field in the spring.

There was no end to the adventures around the school building. It had an incinerator that the janitor used for burning all of the school's trash (these

Living Then & Now

devices are not allowed today: they create way too much pollution). After incineration, the janitor would put the ashes in large barrels every week so the city could haul them away. We kids would dumpster-dive the barrels for treasures. Not much was left except ashes but the big finds were the leftovers of large light bulbs. Every lamp in the building used incandescent light bulbs and they periodically burned out. The janitor would throw them directly into the trash where they'd explode in the incinerator. What was left after the bulbs exploded looked like a miniature antenna and we'd retrieve these, marvel at them, and play with them.

Another area for exploration was along the chain link fence that ran from the south end of the school grounds to the north end on one side. We'd often find treasures along the fence and one day I found a $5 bill. This was big money back then, and I turned it in to the school office. They announced it over the loudspeaker system that "someone had found a large amount of money" and whoever did, could claim it in the principal's office. No one did so I became $5 richer.

In winter, I don't know what the girls were doing, but the boys' main fun was playing army. The older boys would recruit large, opposing armies from all the available male students. Then the "soldiers" would make guns out of snow. At the appropriate time, the armies would charge and fight one another. The charging kids' many feet pounded so hard on the ground it sounded like horses' hooves. This was safe fun; no one got hurt tackling and wrestling one another in the snow.

If we misbehaved, the schoolyard supervisors, a husband and wife team, would line us up along the fence for a time-out.

We had an on-site nurse five days a week at school, also. If you scraped your knee playing outside or if you didn't feel well, you'd end up in the nurse's room and she'd fix you up.

In summer, when school was not in session, the school was open anyway for games and other fun. On Friday nights, the school sponsored "Fun Night," where the parents would bring their kids to the school and the kids would play games and participate in other activities.

Other Boyhood Friends

A neighbor Bob had thousands of plastic army figures. Some from the Civil War, some from World War II. We would construct opposing "forts" for these men out of wooden blocks, place the men inside and outside the forts. Then, when the "war" started, we'd throw old D-size batteries as projectiles at each other's forts in an attempt to win the war. Whoever had the most army men standing when the battle was over, won.

Living Then & Now

My friend Jack's mother was an artist, thus she always had large rolls of paper around the house. Jack and I drew cities, rivers, bridges, buildings, houses, everything on rolls of this paper, which were perhaps three feet broad and of course were almost unlimited in length. We created the cities of our fantasies using pencil and paper.

Jack also had a subscription to Mad Magazine, and his older sister had records that turned us on to more "mature" sounds. These included La Bamba by Richie Valens (B side, Oh Donna), Sea of Love by Phil Phillips, Elvis Presley records, and others.

We were into inventing things, testing things, building things. We invented an underwater experiment for ants. It consisted of a glass bottle wherein we put food for the ants, corked the bottle, and attached a breathing tube. Before school we put the bottle in the creek near Jack's house. After school, we retrieved the bottle, and, great! The ants were still alive!

We also buried treasures. Into a cardboard box we put various items and buried the box in the earth. After a few weeks we unearthed the box but found out the moisture destroyed the box and most of the contents.

We fabricated parachutes out of old pillowcases and used D batteries to weigh down the ends. This worked well and we had a good time throwing these up in the air and watching them land.

Kites were big, too. We bought kites cheaply from the five and dime store, both the triangular models and box kites. We flew them mostly in Spring when the winds were high, and we attached as much string to them as possible, so much string that it weighed down the center and therefore required an hour to reel the kite back in.

We built model cars out of plastic kits we bought from the hobby store, but were not satisfied with only the design the kit provided so we modified the vehicles. A friend showed me that you could light plastic with a match or lighter and it would melt, so one could shape it and also make parts. We made extra parts like bumpers and roll bars for the kit cars. After we were through creating these modified cars, we'd often attach a string to them and tie the other end onto our bikes. Then we'd drag the car down the road. We'd also have demolition derbies with the cars until we destroyed them or made them only usable for parts.

A section of land near Jack's house was undeveloped. It was a large field with grasses and buckhorn sumac. We called it "Quail Meadow." I stole an arrowhead from my father's bow and arrow set. We attached it to a hard, long reed to create a spear. We never speared anything and never saw a quail, either.

Fishing in the Menomonee River was hopeless because it was so polluted, but that did not prevent us from spending hours playing and exploring the land and woods along the banks and the creek that fed it. We walked the path that ran along the river, we caught crawfish, we skated on it in winter. We had hours of fun at the "car wash." This was an area of the river where at one time a company which was mining Lannon stone near the river built a shortcut for trucks across the water by placing large pieces of the stone into the river so trucks could use the stones as a bridge to the other side, greatly reducing the distance to the highway. The company long ago stopped mining the stone but the bridge-like stones were still there so one could walk across the river to the other side. We also had fun on the bridge, as it allowed us to be in the middle of the current so we could watch the water flow by.

Girls

In the fifth and sixth grades, the boys and girls began to discover one another. The school had dances after school periodically, and parents would also allow their kids to have private parties in their homes. These were usually sweaty affairs, especially the private parties where the slow-dance records allowed the boys and girls to come into close physical contact. Not that discovering the opposite sex changed much in our lives; it didn't.

Living Then & Now

But the awareness began and became more influential as we matured.

Moving on from grade school to junior high school (now middle school) was a big deal. Not only did all of us as a group move to a different school, one that was also miles away from home for many of the students, but now instead of remaining in one room throughout the day, we moved to different rooms for different classes, which somehow made us feel more grown up.

Getting to school and getting home was an adventure in itself. My neighborhood friend's mother worked as a secretary at one of the high schools in our district. She drove to her school every day and dropped me and her son, and later my brother, off on a road that was half-way to the junior high school. From there we'd catch a city bus the remainder of the way. After school, we'd catch the same bus going in the opposite direction, but we'd have to transfer to another bus, which dropped us off five and one-half blocks from home. So there was a lot of walking and waiting. Often the buses on the afternoon shift were extremely crowded, to the point where there was no more room and we'd have to wait for the next one, further delaying our arrival home.

Living Then & Now

It was in some respects easier to get home if you had an after-school activity. The buses were far less crowded. Of course, the downside was that you'd arrive home even later than a normal school day. My extracurricular activities were football and swimming, depending on the time of year. Football in autumn, swimming in winter.

As devious children will sometimes do, we found a way to use the bus fare our parents gave us for candy and treats. Every week the bus company issued student passes, which we bought at a discount. The passes retained the same design every week but changed colors. As many weeks as we could, we'd find out what the color combination was for the week, use our little scissors and glue or tape, and create a new, bogus bus pass out of previous passes. We'd then place the "new' pass in a bus pass holder, and viola, we'd have a free bus pass for the current week. I never heard of anyone getting caught making and using a fake bus pass.

Another nefarious activity we engaged in was filing down pennies. My family belonged to a swim club, actually part of a large bowling alley facility. Inside the bowling alley were pinball machines. My friends and I would spend many hours scraping pennies on the concrete sidewalk outside of the place, filing the pennies down until they were the size of dimes. Then we would go inside the bowling alley and play the 10 cent pinball machines.

I was rarely fortunate. In my growing up years, I had friends from way more than my immediate neighborhood. Because I attended a junior high school that was far away, in addition to the neighborhood buddies I got to know kids from the neighborhood where the junior high school was located. As a result of my family belonging to the swim club, I became acquainted with the group of kids who lived around the club. Later on, because of a job I held for a couple of years, I got to know kids from around the neighborhood where I worked.

About half the members of our swim club were Jewish. Of course, as kids, we did not know that and in fact could not have cared less. We only were looking for friends to hang out with. For the record, I became friends with Steve Marcus. Steve's family owned the Big Boy restaurant chain in our area and eventually owned a hotel chain and a theatre chain. Another friend was Bill Fazio, the son of the owners of Fazio's Italian Restaurant, a popular downtown Milwaukee restaurant.

Bands

I was always trying to start a rock 'n roll band when I was a teenager. Remember, this was the time of the "British invasion," and nearly all kids wanted to be a member of a band. I had taught myself how to play guitar and got a job so I could buy an electric instrument. I concentrated on playing rhythm guitar.

Living Then & Now

My friend Bob also played guitar and he was a lead guitar player, in other words, he could play solos whereas my role was to supply the rhythm, a danceable background to help keep the rhythm and the beat. Bob and I tried out a few drummers to back us up but nothing seemed to gel. Then I got an idea. I knew of another group of boys who were also attempting to start a band. I thought: why not join our two groups? Their group consisted of a drummer, a boy who played guitar and sang, and another boy who sang and played tambourine. We got together at the drummer's parents' house, and it worked. The two groups, when joined together, gelled and we had a rock band. We named the group The Rising Tide and began practicing earnestly at the drummer's house.

Band members were: Bob and I, Gary, the other singer and guitarist; Bruce, the drummer; and Jeff (nick named "Binky") who sang and played tambourine. The idea was to have Jeff be the bass player but we never had enough money to buy him a bass guitar.

In fact, we had very little in the way of equipment. Bob, Gary, and I each had our own guitars. Bob had his own amplifier, and an old accordion amplifier powered mine. Gary and Jeff ran Gary's guitar and their microphones through a Sears Silvertone amplifier. That was it.

Living Then & Now

We did have one advantage over some other groups: the brother of our lead guitarist was an artist. To identify the band, he designed a colorful, tasteful Rising Tide insert for the bass drum.

After rehearsing and getting our songs down well, we auditioned for and then landed our first "gig," the St. Valentine's Day dance at our junior high school. This was the big event of the year and so it was quite an accomplishment to procure that opportunity to play.

The dance, held in the school's gymnasium, was wall-to-wall students and a grand success.

Around this time, the local YMCA sponsored a "battle of the bands." It consisted of a contest between the Rising Tide and only one other band. That band was made up of the smart, A students from school and they had nicer equipment and even a bass player. But we won that battle, so we must have been pretty good.

Our next objective was the "Y" dance. This was a once-a-month, Friday night dance that the local YMCA sponsored. If you were big locally, you played the Y dance; all the popular, more well-equipped, and talented bands played this dance.

We thought we might have a chance so we asked the band that was the entertainment one Friday night if we could play during their break. The

Living Then & Now

members of The Dimensions looked at us like we were crazy amateurs, but I guess they figured they had nothing to lose, so they let us play. Of course we got to use their instruments, amplifiers, drum set, etc. Fender amplifiers, great guitars and drum set helped us sound fantastic. The YMCA management was duly impressed and so we secured a Y dance date.

The dance went well. We played our little hearts out and the people danced like crazy. When we ran through our song list, we just started over. The audience could not have cared less about hearing the songs twice. They just kept dancing.

Eventually, after we conquered the two big gigs, the St. Valentine's Day Dance and the Y Dance, the band broke up. I do not believe any of us had dreams of making a career out of being in a band or even being professional musicians, so breaking up was natural and inevitable.

Soon it was time to move on to high school. In those days in our school system, middle school was 7th, 8th, and 9th grades. Nineth grade is normally considered a student's freshman year in high school, so by the time we entered high school, we were actually sophomores.

The high school was located nearer to my home, in fact only about half the distance, so if necessary, my fellow classmates and I could walk to and from

Living Then & Now

school. But even so, it was a two-mile trip so we either got a ride to school from the same neighbor who took us half-way to the junior high, another adult, or we took the bus.

A couple hundred yards from the high school was a Big Boy coffee shop, which turned out to be a place to hang out before, after, and sometimes during school. Railroad tracks paralleled the school grounds and at the time, no tunnel underneath the tracks existed, as there is today, so students crossed over the tracks to get to the highway that ran near the school or to Big Boy. Many students crossed the tracks, especially before and after school, but no one ever got hurt as far as I know.

The high school building itself was, we found out later, designed to be a junior high. But because of the great need for another high school, it served that purpose until the district could build a new high school, which they did a few years hence. Our class was supposed to be the first class to graduate from the new edifice but the building was vandalized during construction, which put off completion for a year.

Pranks and Protests

One of the pranks us high schoolers were going to implement was a prank during a school assembly. When the administration called the students

Living Then & Now

together for a significant announcement, a pep rally, or some other reason, they gathered us all together in the gymnasium. (The school did not have an auditorium.) And whenever they gathered us together, they always played the National Anthem on a record player to start the event. The record player broadcasted the song over the loudspeaker system in the gym. The plan my friends and I had was to put a different record ("Hey Jude" by the Beatles) on the turntable in place of the National Anthem record.

A couple of friends and I sneaked up near the school principal who stood near the record player, ready to play the Star Spangled Banner. We had our record in hand. The timing had to be right for us to grab the National Anthem record and replace it with our record right before he played the recording. Well, we missed by about 30 seconds.

We perpetuated pranks outside of school, too. When a person received a phone call at the swim club my family belonged to, one of the staff would use the public address system to announce that they had a phone call and to please come to the main desk to answer it. One of my friends lived just a few doors away from the club facilities and we could easily hear these announcements from my friend's bedroom window. For some fun, we'd call the club and ask for fictitious people like Mike Rafone,

Living Then & Now

Chuck Wagon, or Hedda Lettuce and have a laugh when they announced the name.

Another phone prank that gave us a laugh, although not fun for the people who answered the phone was this: we'd randomly call a number. When someone answered we'd say, "This is the bus company calling. Did you take a bus this week?" If the person answered, yes, we'd say, "Give it back!" and hang up. Or we'd ask, "Is your refrigerator running?" If they answered, yes, we'd say, "Better go catch it!"

What small things amuse young kids.

Protest

In May 1970, when we were in our senior year in high school, the Vietnam War was raging. The National Guard had recently killed five student protesters on the Kent State college campus. My friends and I had had enough of these terrible political tragedies. We decided to stage a walkout in protest of the expanding war and the horrible campus killings. Five or six of us, including an artist friend, met in the basement of my parents' house. We planned a 9:00 a.m. strike on a Friday at the school, complete with black arm bands made from black socks, posters, and opportunities for discussion and dissension. Before the event, our artist friend drew up posters the read "Strike!" with a clenched fist graphic, and also leaflets designed to

Living Then & Now

inform the student body of the strike. We engaged a former student, an African American (one of the few who lived in our suburb) to present a talk about the war and what was happening in the country.

We arrived on that Friday morning all set to conduct a peaceful walkout only to find that some other students had graffitied the school. Feeling betrayed and with some of the wind knocked out of our sails, we decided the strike must go on. At 9:00 a.m., more than half the student body walked out of classes and onto the front lawn of the school. Soon, some of the teachers and administrators joined us and eventually classes were cancelled for the day.

Small groups formed as we discussed and sometimes argued about the war and other important issues of the day, such as race relations, fair housing, school dress codes, etc.

Because he was not an administrator, teacher, or current student, the school administration would not allow our African American speaker onto the school property to give his talk, so we gathered a short distance from the school and listened to him speak.

With classes shut down and most of the students and high school staff out on the lawn in front of the school, we considered the strike a success.

Very few in our group attended football games or the prom. I went out for football but stopped after

Living Then & Now

my sophomore year. I recall watching some of the seniors practice. It looked rough. Remember, back then there were no penalties for roughing the quarterback or personal fouls. In fact, as a sophomore, the quarterback on my team, who happened to be Bob, the former lead guitarist in my band, was sacked by three or four big linemen and when they lifted the linemen off of the pile, found that Bob had a broken arm in three places. I saw it: what was once a straight arm now looked like a twisted, beat up piece of flesh.

I did go to one dance. The dance was called "Turnabout," which meant the girls asked the boys, the opposite of what usually happened. I went with my steady girlfriend at the time, Kathy, and we doubled with another couple, driving my Dad's car a 1967 Buick Le Sabre, to and from the event.

My friends and I did occasionally cut class, especially when we were seniors, but when we were caught over at Big Boys and given demerits, we found out it was not worth it. So we ploughed on and eventually graduated. My friends and I were actually pretty good students and planned on attending college.

With high school finally over, my friend Scott and I decided to room together at the University of Wisconsin-Madison, where we were both accepted.

Living Then & Now

Our dads together drove us to the campus and registered us for classes and for housing in a dormitory (living in a dorm was required for first year students). It turned out, the freshman class advisors registered us for all the early classes (the upper classmen wanted to sleep in), so that was strike one in our minds. The dormitory was a small, 15 X 10 room with two single beds and a desk in between. The communal shower was down the hall, and the cafeteria served institutional food.

Doing our best to be good students, we went to the early classes, lived in the dorm together, and ate the dormitory food. It was doable. What was not doable was the weekend activities. On our first weekend on campus, we experienced the abject drinking and drunkenness of the students. We were invited to party and when we did, we found students passed, dead drunk, sprawled out in the hallways of various buildings on campus. We were also astonished to discover they still had panty raids. Combined, these were too much.

So we planned our escape. Scott's parents had purchased a car for him, an Austin Healy Sprite, which was a small, convertible, two-seater sports car. We announced to our parents we were dropping out of college, and promised to attend the local University of Wisconsin campus in Milwaukee the next semester.

Living Then & Now

After we officially notified the university that we were dropping out, we received our refund, which gave us some money, and we proceeded with our plan. First, we drove Scott's little car back and forth between Milwaukee and Madison a few times so we could remove our meager possessions and transport them to my parent's house, which would be our temporary living situation for the remainder of the first semester.

In the meantime, we got busy implementing the next phases of our plan. The idea was to rent a house near the UW-Milwaukee campus, furnish it with furniture and other items from second-hand stores, and invite friends to occupy the house with us to save on rent. Then we'd enroll in classes for the second semester, After that, we'd see what happened.

It worked OK. We bought beds, kitchen and living room furniture from St. Vincent De Paul's and three friends readily accepted rooming in the other three rooms of the five-bedroom house. My parent's donated an old China dish set they weren't using and we set up a schedule for cooking and cleaning, dividing up the household chores between the five roommates.

For income, we were going to be pot dealers. This may sound dangerous but, in the day, this was fairly normal. Four of the five house members were experienced pot sellers because we had sold pot in

Living Then & Now

high school. Also, the police at the time were not serious about prosecuting pot dealers and most young people smoked pot, so a ready market existed.

So, we were off. We followed the schedule, we sold enough pot to pay the rent, and we even found an additional housemate in the form of my older sister, who convinced my dad to build here a room in the attic of the house.

All ran well for about six months. It was the substance dealing that was doing us in. The dealing went from pot to hashish, then on to, psychedelics, cocaine and even heroin. I wanted out. So did my sister. In fact, after about six months, she and I moved out together. I'm not sure where my sister moved to; I moved back in with my parent's home temporarily.

After High School

After I moved out of the "hippie" house, I stayed with my parents for a while but it seemed like my life was going nowhere. My girlfriend Denise and I were pretty close so I had this idea that we could get married. She agreed but a little issue developed about when. I wanted to get married soon but her parents wanted us to wait and have a *real* wedding. This did not work for me so Denise and I one day arranged to go to the courthouse to marry. A minor glitch there (I do not remember what it was) but after the county ironed it out, the judge married us.

We went to my new in-law's house to announce that we were married. Denise's grandfather declared we had eloped, which I guess we did, and he and I toasted the event. My parents and Denise's later worked out the details for a reception a couple of months down the road, so the celebration part was fixed. In the meantime, we hired a caterer, printed invitations, engaged a band, and rented a hall. At the event, both sides of our families attended, along with my friends and Denise's friends, and our marriage was complete.

We rented a small apartment -- coincidentally just down the block from the hippie house, although I did not venture there after I was married -- for $97 a month. My sister and her boyfriend gave us a car for a wedding present, one that had seen better days but which ran and got us where we needed to go.

Actually, we did not really need the car. Where we lived on Milwaukee's East Side, one could walk or bike to grocery stores and other places like bars and the laundromat. It remains so today. For my wife and I, the living was relatively easy, although at first neither of us had a job. Eventually Denise got a job as a clerk at Gimbels department store and I got a job pumping gas at a gas station. We made ends meet and continued seeing our friends and hanging out.

Living Then & Now

But it was getting boring, working these menial jobs and going nowhere. I wanted a bigger place and to be away from the East Side, so I found a two-bedroom place in the suburb of Wauwatosa and we moved. I got a job as an assistant manager of a shoe store and Denise moved on to a job as a receptionist at a manufacturing company. I also enrolled back in college at the University of Wisconsin-Milwaukee campus, for a couple of classes.

After a year or so, the boredom and tediousness of our life set in. Then I got the idea to move to Madison, Wisconsin, home of the flagship University of Wisconsin-Madison campus and the state capitol. We took a trip there, liked what we saw, and rented a cute apartment. In a couple of weeks we were out of Milwaukee and residing in Madison.

In the area we moved to in Madison, the rent was doable. If one moves away from campus, the housing, at least at that time, was reasonable, lower than the rent prices in Milwaukee.

Madison had a markedly different feel than Milwaukee. It was more small town for one, but the major difference was that it was not so working class -- the dollar bill wasn't the main objective in everyone's mind. Also the population was quite eclectic; people came from all over the U.S. and many parts of the world to attend school there.

This was great, in my mind. I could get to know people from all over and at the same time, not be so immediately concerned about finding a permanent job and a career path.

But I did have to find work, we both did, in order to pay the rent and put food on the table. Denise landed a part time job at a plant store at East Towne mall, functioning as assistant manager. At first, I could not find anything, try as I might. The economy was in a recession (this was the early 1970's) and jobs were scarce. Finally, I got a job as a school bus driver. I did that for a year, two semesters. The pay was fair and I enjoyed being with the kids, grade schoolers through high school. But it involved a lot of driving, not so much actually driving the bus but driving twice a day, five days a week to and from the bus depot, which was located just outside of Madison in Sun Prairie, Wisconsin. The drive there and back was 20 minutes each way. I carpooled with two other drivers from Madison to save money.

After my year of school bus driving ended, I noticed that a photo developing store and shop just a block from our apartment had a Help Wanted sign in the window. I inquired, interviewed, and they hired me -- as a delivery driver (more driving) two days a week. I also signed up for a couple of courses at UW.

Living Then & Now

Needless to say, we kept busy. After a few months of delivery driving, the facility manager at the photo shop brought me into the plant and trained me as a filmstrip and slide duplicator. This meant I duplicated filmstrips for industry. These presentations provided information to customers, students, and workers about dairy farming, plant management, driver education, whatever. I also duplicated slides for retail customers, for example, if a family member wanted slides from a wedding. Remember, this was way before Power Point or digital cameras.

So now I had a skilled job.

Denise signed up for courses at the local technical college, and left the plant store job to become a bank teller, full time.

Also, the couple who managed the building we lived in told us they were moving back to New York City where they were from and asked me to take over the job. For the maintenance and rental duties, we received a reduction in rent. I accepted, so now I had two jobs plus university classes.

Madison's population is only about a quarter of that of Milwaukee's, and it's situated on five lakes. So it was pleasant while we lived there to be able enjoy the lakes and the parks and to bike or walk to places.

Living Then & Now

Well, after a few years, I was getting restless again. Eventually I asked Denise if she would move back to Milwaukee. She did not want to – she had a good job, a nice apartment, friends. I liked the apartment, and had friends, too, but I couldn't take Madison anymore. It was not a "grounded" place to live. The people, students, government workers, teachers -- often they only live there for a short time, for example while attending school or when elections change the state government and new people come in to take the administrative jobs. Milwaukee was more stable. I know that this was the exact opposite of my thinking before we moved to Madison but that's how I operated back then – trying to follow my feelings.

So when my wife declined to move, I left anyway. Back in Milwaukee, I got a job at a photo development company, similar to what I was doing in Madison. I worked there for a while but was not happy. Increasingly, my responsibilities were developing film. At that time, developing film involved handling and working with a lot of chemicals, which did not appeal to me at all. So I was on the lookout for a better job.

An advertisement in the newspaper said a job opening existed at Harley-Davidson Motor Company, the company that made motorcycles. I remember consciously thinking I needed to feel more macho and maybe working at a place like that would help me to feel that way. So I applied for the position.

The ad was rather unspecific about what the job entailed but I did not care. I was looking for full-time employment at a fair salary with normal business hours. This job at least had that, I found out because they interviewed me. Long story short, they hired me and I began work in the Sales Department at Harley. The other new hire, Pat, and I shared a makeshift office in the conference room of the department. Each of us had a phone with which we were to contact all the dealers in the network each week to find out what was in their inventory.

Needless to say, the dealers were not crazy about the idea of revealing their inventory to us, especially if their sales were not good. But, when we told the dealer upon getting him (all the dealers were men) on the phone that we were calling from "the factory," this made them, grudgingly, want to cooperate. They eventually became used to us calling them and some even became almost friendly.

After six months of phone inventory work, the department manager told us the job was over. I thought I'd be looking for another job, but, no, they offered both of us opportunities in other departments. Pat took a job as a secretary in the Engineering Department. I took a job as a Data

Living Then & Now

Base Clerk in the Service Department. So, I remained working, with a good salary and no weird hours.

Denise and I were moving in separate directions in life. She was happy with her living situation, her job, and her friends. I had discovered yoga and meditation and was working hard at making progress in both and also becoming active in the local group activities. She eventually filed for divorce, which was fine with me, and soon I was a single person again.

I was making new friends, mostly through the yoga group, and enjoying it. We'd meet every Thursday evening for a meditation service and often go out for coffee or food afterwards. So we had opportunities to bond. My friend Rose was a widow with five grown children. Mike had graduated in Social Work and was determined to land a job in his field. John had graduated and was now in Graduate School learning to be a counselor.

Rose worked full time as a secretary for a large company, so she and I were rather on the same schedule: working Monday through Friday with weekends off. Now and then it was only Rose and I getting together after the Thursday event and it amazed me that she was always willing to seek out a late-night restaurant. She often stated, "I'm always hungry after meditation!" That worked for me because I always enjoyed going out for food.

Living Then & Now

My living situation was rather chaotic. After landing the job at Harley, I moved into a studio apartment within (long) walking distance to my office. I stayed there until I received an offer from another friend, George, who owned a home only a few blocks from my office. This was another studio apartment with a shared bathroom. But it was cheap and very near work, so I took it.

I got used to a routine. Working Monday through Friday, doing things socially with the meditation group, and occasionally going out on dates. I soon got the data base in order in the Service Department at my job and so, in addition to continuing to maintain the data base on a daily basis, my boss had me processing warranty claims. Many claims hit the department in those days – ask any Harley owner. The quality of the vehicles at that time was probably at an all-time low. In fact many of the employees who were motorcycle riders rode Kawasakis or Hondas to and from work, which the Harley employees would probably consider a cardinal sin today. But things were looking up. A group of businessmen, which included the grandson of one of the founders, eventually bought the company from AMF Corporation, the company that had owned Harley-Davidson for a few years and which many owners blamed for the poor products. The new owners were introducing new models and making an effort to improve quality.

Living Then & Now

As a warranty processor, database clerk and with a few other responsibilities like selling used motors and serving as a liaison between our department and the IT area, I had plenty to do. But it was boring. I had been working this job for four years and, unless I had serious thoughts about becoming a permanent part of the Harley company, which I didn't, I considered the job a dead end. I also realized that people who had a university degree got the better jobs. When a man became my boss who I did not respect, I decided to quit and return to college full-time to complete my studies and get my degree.

So, after giving my notice and taking a little time off including a small vacation, I began to rearrange my life and to gather the tools I would need so I could return to school. This included downsizing my living situation. I moved into a three-bedroom flat with two others to save rent money and reduce other living expenses. I also had a rummage sale where I sold things I didn't need, including a car someone had given me, a hide-a-bed, and some other personal items that were extras.

Just as important, I went to the University and sat down with a financial advisor with regards to financing three years of college education, which was approximately the amount of time I needed to get my bachelor's degree. The advisor was knowledgeable and helpful. He told me about student loans that were available, which I did not need to pay back until after graduation. These loans were available through the federal government and were quite low interest. We also discussed grants and on-campus work opportunities. From the way the advisor described them, I was not interested in the available grants but I was interested in the job opportunities, which he said were many. After the meeting I had all the information and forms I needed to apply for student loans and I had a plan to seek out part-time employment so I could avoid as much debt as possible.

While on campus, I obtained a schedule of the classes the University was offering in the Fall so I could get an idea of which classes I wanted to take. My plan was to go to school full-time, taking 12 credits, and work part-time, hopefully on campus to avoid spending time travelling off campus to a job. I looked over all the classes they were offering in almost every department, except for the obvious ones like Nursing, Social Work, and Engineering, etc., which I had no interest in. The idea was to discover any courses which I might find interesting, since I had not decided on a major course of study yet.

When the following autumn rolled around, I was all set. I had my living situation in order, my finances lined up so I could pay for living expenses, tuition, and books, and, most importantly, I had set my

Living Then & Now

mind on doing what was required for the next three years to complete college and get my degree.

The situation with the roommates did not work out (two of them moved on with their lives), so I rented a small apartment near campus, but not too near where I'd be paying exorbitant rent just to be close to school. The apartment was on a bus line, which enabled me to travel there in about 10 minutes. That was close enough.

I also landed a job on campus in the International Student Office, a division of the University's Office of the Registrar, which is the office responsible for processing applications and registering students for entrance to the University. My job was processing applications for international students interested in attending the University of Wisconsin-Milwaukee. When a student made an initial application, they had to include the application form itself, an application fee, proof of a valid student visa, and transcripts, both high school and any college transcripts. My duty was to make sure the applications were complete and to notify the applicant if the University required any additional materials. I could schedule my work around my classes so the office allowed me the freedom to come and go as needed.

The plan began to work and I began to work the plan. I was enjoying my classes and my job was interesting. I took classes in the departments of

Living Then & Now

Economics, Communication, English, Film, and History, which gave me an idea what a career in those fields would be like. It turned out the I was most attracted to the English Department (no surprise there, really, since I had had an interesting in writing and books even before high school). So after a couple of semesters I became an English major. Bear in mind that I did not know at all what I wanted to do in life as a career when I started college. Experimenting by taking classes in various fields helped me discriminate between choices.

The job was changing because the International Student Office was changing. In short, because of some administrative vicissitudes, the department ceased being a division of the Office of the Registrar and became part of the Graduate School. As a result, I knew people in the Registrar's office but soon became acquainted with administrators, deans, and students in the Graduate School. In the upper administration of the University, the administrators and instructors often wore a couple of "hats." For example, one of my professors in the English Department was also a dean in the Graduate School.

Due to training in one of my classes, I became an editor, and soon international students were asking me to edit their papers, theses, and even dissertations, for which they paid me. I volunteered to edit three newsletters that came out of my office,

Living Then & Now

and also got a job for a couple of semesters as a writer and producer of a campus radio program. Little did I know it, but I was receiving hands-on training in my field that would help me in future endeavors.

Another fortuitous opportunity came my way as I worked my way through college. I only took a class or two during summer and I was only working part-time on campus, so I had some time that I thought I could use profitably. I planned to write to some local publishing companies to see if they needed any help. I had time to send off only one letter to one company but the editor of a magazine at that company called me and wanted to hire me as a part-time copy editor. So for a summer, I worked at a publishing company, gaining more experience, and making some money doing it.

It was nearing the time for me to graduate. I had the required number of credits for this, or so I thought, and planned to graduate in May 1983 with a degree in English. A problem arose with this plan, and I had to schedule a meeting with the head of the English department, Professor Chang. At the meeting, Dr. Change looked over my records, filled out a form, and bingo, I was set.

I attended the graduation ceremony at the Milwaukee Auditorium, a big arena-type gathering place and stepped up onto the platform to receive my degree. Finally, thirteen years after graduating

Living Then & Now

from high school, it was over. I was done with school, at least for a while.

I figured I had my job and other editing work at the University, so why not apply to Graduate School in the English Department. I did this but, it didn't work out. Even though I completed the requirements and my grades were adequate, I was not accepted into the graduate program. So, in order to pursue a master's degree seriously, I'd have to apply to other schools in the United States. I was not that intent about graduate school – the only reason I applied was to remain working at the University, so it would have been a convenient situation. But it was not to be.

At this time, I became involved with a young woman from my meditation group who had an eight-year-old son. Another long story short, we became romantically involved and eventually we married. She lived in Kenosha, Wisconsin, about 60 miles south of where I was living in Milwaukee, and owned a small house there. We agreed that I would give up my apartment and share the house.

I moved in with Kristin and her son Sean and began to commute to my part-time job at the University. It was the only employment I had at the time, so I did the commute. But the drive was grueling even though I sometimes car-pooled with another commuter, and eventually it became too much. So I resigned and began to look for work closer to home.

Living Then & Now

I began doing odd jobs around the town, and on the way home from one of them, I stopped at the "guard shack" at a one of the big businesses in Kenosha, Snap-on Tools. The company's world headquarters is in Kenosha and it has a large campus of offices and manufacturing there (manufacturing has since stopped at that location). I talked to the guard about working there and he handed me an application for employment. I filled it out, handed it back to him, and proceeded to make my way home.

A few days later, a woman from Snap-on called me, and asked if I could come in for an interview. I was happily surprised. I knew the company made tools for the automotive industry but did not give much thought when I was filling out the application as to how I might fit in there. I just thought I could perhaps get a job of some sort.

When I arrived for the interview, the greeter showed me into an office in the personnel department. Inside a woman named Jan greeted me cordially. I sat down and we began to talk. The conversation turned to writing and she informed me she was the author of several children's books. I had been working on two children's books myself so that is how the topic came up.

After two days passed, Jan called me and offered me a job. In my mind, this was great. I'd have a steady income, normal working hours, and be close

Living Then & Now

to home. I accepted. She asked me to report for work the following day, which I did.

When I arrived, I sat down with Jan again and she went over the details about the salary and the benefits. I did not quibble about the salary because at the time it was entirely an employer work environment: what they offered, you accepted. Of course, the job came with complete benefits, medical, dental, paid time off, and enrollment in the retirement program. This was normal for all employees. Next, Jan walked me over to the department where I was going to be working, the Advertising Department, and introduced me to my new boss, Rick.

Rick walked me around the department, showing me the writers' area, the artists' area, and the photo studio. After my department tour, my new boss said work started at 7:30 a.m. and ended at 4:30 p.m. with an hour lunch. He then said, "See you tomorrow at 7:30" and bid me goodbye.

When I arrived home, it began to dawn on me that I'd be working in advertising. I had not really thought about it before then, just that it was a job. This was all new to me. My job title was Copywriter and it occurred to me that I landed the job in part because I had some experience at the University writing and editing but also because I had created a brochure there for new international students, a copy of which I had included with my job application.

On my first day, I sat down with one of the staff writers and he began to teach me about how to design and draft a catalog page, a page in the company's tool catalog. This was my introduction to the many and varied types of assignments and projects I was to work on as a copywriter. Eventually those included four-color brochures, press releases, training materials, audio-visual presentations, and videos, among others.

Without getting into too much detail, writing and producing audio-visual programs and videos required that I write the script, secure the products and the props, work with the photographer or videographer, create the soundtrack and produce the narration (for audio-visual productions), and now and then be an actor in the production. These tasks were in addition to working with the client (the department head or product manager) supervising the shoot, and working with a vendor for packaging and distribution.

Former military personnel ran Snap-on; many of the administrators and managers were former World War II military. My boss at the publishing company I worked for briefly was a former Marine and some of the older employees and some management at Harley-Davidson were former military. I mention this because the people in management areas of

Living Then & Now

these companies ran them like a military organization. Starting time at Snap-on was 7:30 a.m., where we had to arrive on time, shoes shined, suit and tie. Women wore skirts and dresses. Lunch began exactly at the prescribed time. You went home at the exact ending time, too, every day. The day was quite regimented.

However, the advertising Department at Snap-on was a little different. We had to report at 7:30 in the morning and dress the part like the other departments, but most of the advertising people sat around drinking coffee and smoking for an hour or so before beginning work. My boss, who was the department supervisor, and his boss, the department manager, were distinctly freedom loving. If we needed more time for a project, no problem. If someone in another department in the company was uncooperative, they went to bat for you. We had a "freedom" board, a bulletin board where anyone in the department could post items of interest. These included pictures, articles, cartoons, jokes – whatever.

Chalk this up perhaps to the fact that we were expected to be creative. The writers, artists, and photographers were expected to present the company's products in a new light, all the time, even though the basic product, ratcheting wrenches and sockets, had really not changed since the founder invented them in the 1920's. So management gave us more leeway in our behavior, our jobs, and our approach to work.

To be fair, the product does go beyond sockets and wrenches. Snap-on makes electronic diagnostic instruments, sophisticated hand tools, such as unique tools for the space program, tools for surgery, and many others. But its main product is hand tools for the automotive industry.

The atmosphere in the office included grey, Steelcase® desks and partitions, and overhead fluorescent lights. We had no windows in our department. Like Harley-Davidson where I worked previously, almost everyone in the office smoked cigarettes. I had quit smoking years ago but no one said anything about the problems associated with second-hand smoke, so non-smokers just had to tolerate the tobacco cloud in most offices.

The artists I mentioned were touch-up artists. They used spray paint and other methods to touch up photographs, which we writers used for advertisements and brochures. They also created artwork for the yearly catalog and any other print project that the department produced. One of the artists even created an entire font for one of my projects.

Included in this group were three, full-time photographers. They worked in their own photo studio and photo development lab where they

Living Then & Now

produced the photos we needed for brochures and other print materials. They also shot the slides for our audio-visual programs.

The writer area, of which I was a member, included two audio-visual writers/producers; three "catalog" writers, who were responsible for writing the copy for and producing the annual printed catalog; two technical writers, who wrote the copy for any technical publications that accompanied the tools and equipment the company produced; and my area, the "collateral" writers, which were me and another writer who did everything that was unusual or that the others did not have time or the wherewithal to do.

In the five years that Snap-on employed me, I learned much about the advertising business, specifically about all the details involved with writing and producing four-color printed materials, and, toward the end of my experience, all about writing and producing audio-visual presentations.

Five years after Snap-on hired me, I was getting to the point where I was done. It was enjoyable being a member of a fun-loving team. But the bottom line was: the company wanted me to spend most of my time in its sound studio, producing audio-visual shows. This meant little writing. My ambition was to write so I felt it was near the time for Snap-on and I to part ways.

In the meantime, my second wife had filed for divorce. That is another long story but to keep it short, she had other plans for her life. So she filed and we got divorced after a short, two year marriage.

I moved from Kenosha to Milwaukee after the divorce with the idea I would commute the 40-mile trip to Kenosha every day; no remote work existed at the time. To be nearer my job, I rented a flat on the city's south side and I asked a friend from my yoga group to move in to help with expenses, which he did.

By the time one gets to the freeway that leads to Kenosha and then gets off and travels to the area of my office at the time, the 40-mile trip turns out to be around an hour. This was on a day when the weather was OK. If it rained or snowed, add more time, so I was spending at least 10 hours in a car every week. Another element was that my car was a big vehicle and burned a lot of gas. Overall, time- and money-wise, commuting by myself was not economically justifiable. So, I joined a carpool. The time element was the same but I saved some money by riding with four others and sharing gas expenses.

It was only a matter of time before I made the decision to live once again in Kenosha. Kenosha

Living Then & Now

then was primarily a working-class town of about 80,000 people.[1] In addition to Snap-on, the city had an American Motors automobile plant, "The Brass" (a company that made brass parts for electronics and other industries), a Simons Mattress plant, and others.

So I lived in my one-bedroom apartment, not really knowing anyone at first except for a friend or two from work. I was dating a lady who lived in Kenosha but she eventually moved to Chicago and we broke up. Living in Kenosha became a lonely existence. One good result was that I again became active in the Milwaukee yoga/meditation group, to which I commuted to the once-a-week Thursday evening meeting.

I felt as if I were looking at a "30-year sentence" at Snap-on. I worked there five years and I was enjoying my job less and less. It paid well and was tolerable but I felt frustrated and bored. As fate would have it, I met a woman at the yoga group who helped me see alternatives.

When I met Karen, I was slated again to attend Snap-on's Year End meetings. The company hosted these meetings annually, which brought the company and its dealer network together. The

---

[1] At present, Keosha, is more of a "bedroom" community to Chicago, since it is only about 65 miles from Chicago and is served by the Metra, a commuter rail service.

Living Then & Now

location was a fancy hotel or resort somewhere in North America. Activities included contests, meetings where management introduced new products, food, and entertainment. Plus corporate camaraderie, with the Snap-on management and dealers hanging out together.

As an audio-visual writer/producer, the company mandated that I attend the week-long meeting and present the "shows" I had created. We four a/v writers/producers had to set up and actually put the shows on screen at various meetings. This meant setting up the meeting room with special lighting and the a/v equipment prior to the meeting and making sure everything worked.

This was after having spent the previous six months writing and producing the shows. The six-month production period included researching the subject, learning about new products (or new twists on traditional products), working with department managers, writing the scripts, supervising the creating of the visuals, programming the sound and visuals, and many other tasks. We had to create quite a few of these shows and we four writers had to share one production studio. So we had to rotate shifts, which meant working overtime and odd hours. The studio was in use 24 hours a day.

I had been to two Year End meetings in the previous years, one in Toronto and one on Marco Island in Florida. In some respects it was glamorous

Living Then & Now

for the writers because the dealers wanted to meet the creators of the shows. But for the most part it was grueling. We had to be present all five days, starting with a 7:30 a.m. breakfast every morning and ending with dinner and entertainment in the evenings, often until 9:00 or 10:00 at night. Of course we did have some time off for relaxation and enjoying ourselves, but it was basically the same work but in an exotic location. Plus, when it was all over for the year and the limo dropped you off at home at 10:00 Sunday evening, the company expected you to be show up for work as usual at 7:30 a.m. Monday morning.

I was not looking forward to another year of this, but Karen, whom I was working with about my career said to me one evening, "Maybe you don't have to go." These few words got the ideas churning in my head. Maybe she was right. Even though I had already produced my shows and the company had already scheduled me for the meetings and bought my plane ticket, maybe alternatives existed. I began to question what I was doing and why I was doing it.

I had started a small business of my own on the side, I called it White Star Ltd., doing basically what I was doing at Snap-on, advertising copywriting, creating advertising materials, etc., but with more writing. Maybe it was time to leave a job

Living Then & Now

I really did not like anymore and branch out on my own.

With Karen's help, literally, since she began to work with me in my home office at White Star Ltd., I made the decision to resign my day job. It was a difficult resolve because I had little in the way of work outside of Snap-on, even though with Karen's help I had a few clients. Just day-to-day living was going to be a substantial change, after having done the same thing every day for five years. But I did it — I handed in my resignation, and after two weeks' notice, left on the exact same day Snap-on hired me five years earlier: November 1st. (Coincidentally, November 1st is my birthday.)

My home office for White Star Ltd. had a land-line telephone, a couple of filing cabinets, and a home-built, Heath Kit computer I had purchased from the son of one of my Snap-on workmates, who had built the computer himself. The computer had no hard drive, and operated off of the large, 5-1/4″ floppy disks in existence at the time and included two software packages: WordStar, word processing, and Account Star, an accounting program. So, from humble beginnings ….

Karen and I became close, and after a whirlwind romance, which included one date, we got married and moved to Milwaukee. There, I began soliciting work from ad agencies and other sources. I landed

Living Then & Now

one or two clients but that was about it. We took odd jobs to keep things going.

In time, I started writing resumes and cover letters for people. I created a flyer with tear-off phone number tabs, and posted it at various venues. While I advertised in the local newspaper, the main advertising outlet was my old school, the University of Wisconsin-Milwaukee campus. One could post flyers on the many bulletin boards in the many campus buildings and the student union. I also posted them at the Milwaukee School of Engineering (MSOE), Alverno College, even laundromats and bus stops and soon began to have a steady income with this. Karen, as a former corporate person like me, began to do career counseling for some of my clients.

Writing resumes and cover letters was not the type of writing I desired but it helped pay the bills. Working with the clients, many of whom were college students out to land their first real jobs, was enjoyable and challenging. I also worked with business people looking for a change and who needed updated documents to shop new opportunities, and with people who wanted to re-enter the job pools. We still used the Heath Kit computer, and set up office space in our flat to interview the clients and to create the resumes and cover letters. We printed the documents on our dot matrix printer and provided the clients with master copies which they could duplicate on a copy machine.

We had clients who were business managers, IT people, production workers, cooks – virtually people from all walks of life. One of our more interesting clients was a roofer. This man needed invoices, estimates, letters, and contracts written, typed, and printed.

We had to move from our flat because of problems with the landlord. On a whim, I researched on-site apartment manager opportunities. The idea was to operate our writing business and live in an apartment rent-free. I found an ad that sounded interesting and after we met with the gentleman who would potentially become our boss, we accepted a one-bedroom unit in a 24-unit building to manage. The building owner covered our rent, cable, phone, and utilities -- even our laundry expenses. The apartment was relatively near the places I advertised the resume/cover letter/writing business, the UW-Milwaukee campus and downtown Milwaukee. In addition to resumes and cover letters, I began to get clients, students from the University, who needed papers edited and typed. I began to realize that I was not limited to resumes but could help anyone who needed words on a page.

With the writing business and extra work around the apartment complex, we began to save money. We took on another building to manage around the corner from our building. In both buildings I was performing maintenance tasks and Karen was handling much of the paperwork involving renting to tenants. Karen was also working on a book idea and had a publisher in Los Angeles interested in the project. In time we had saved quite a bit of money.

Needless to say, we were busy. In addition to my writing business, Karen had expanded her counseling business. The building around the corner more than tripled our workload, to the point where I felt we needed a place to retreat. My idea was to find a place where we could write and also relax on the weekends. So, I took a trip to the downtown library and began to research places. I found a couple of them and made some inquiries by phone when I returned home. One place was a house in Door County, Wisconsin, situated right on Lake Michigan in a secluded area. It sounded nice so Karen and I, with our dog Christmas, drove the three hours one Saturday to the house to meet the owner.

When we arrived, we were delighted to behold a beautiful fully furnished, three-bedroom, three bath, ranch style home situated right on the shore of Lake Michigan. The immediate area was mostly woods. I had envisioned a "cabin in the woods, and this was way more than that.

Karen and I had a miscommunication. She thought we were looking for a place to get away full-time. I was looking for a weekend retreat. The owner was enquiring as to whether we could occupy his house from September 1 through May; he and his family used the place during the summer. After we discussed and meditated about this, and made sure the owner was OK with the dog, it came to us to take it. Now, after years of working the writing business plus three busy years as apartment managers, we were off to a writers' sabbatical in the woods.

We realized after we moved to the Door County house, that we really needed a break, which we took for the first few weeks at our retreat. Then we began working on a couple of books. Writing resumes and cover letters was impossible since there was no one in the area to write them for. Karen continued working on her book idea, I began work on a book of poetry.

The nine-month retreat flew by fast and soon it was time to leave. Not knowing exactly where we were going to go, we put most of our belongings in storage, then got into the car and we were off, to places known and unknown. First we spent some time with Karen's mother in Pennsylvania where she lived. We also visited my father and stepmother in Georgia, and finally ended up staying with my mother in Milwaukee for a while.

At this point, a writing career was taking a back seat to just being able to support ourselves in some way.

Living Then & Now

Living temporarily in Milwaukee was not going to work for much longer. One day, feeling lost and frustrated, I took the dog down to the Lake Michigan shore, praying and meditating until I received a vision, I finally saw my own resume with the words Technical Writer on the top.

As my position at Snap-on had given me quite a bit of an opportunity to work in the Technical Writing area, where I created brochures for electronic diagnostic equipment and highly complex and sophisticated tools, I was no stranger to dealing with technology, mechanics, and electronics.

I immediately returned home and typed up my new Technical Writer resume. The newspaper contained a number of ads for Tech Writer positions, so I mailed a few of my resumes. Not more than a day passed when I received a phone call from a placement agency who wanted me to interview. I did so promptly and quickly landed my first Technical Writing job, which paid quite well.

I was back working 40 hours at a manufacturing company, very busy writing and illustrating a backlog of operator manuals for the equipment they made. I did this for three years. In the meantime we went for almost living in our car to purchasing our first house. Times were good but I found myself again longing to leave the corporate world. The universe granted my wish. Because I had finished all the work that I had at the company and because I could see that the company was now experiencing a downturn, I was not surprised when my boss called me into his office one morning and explained to me that the company was giving me a "permanent layoff." In other words, I was out of a job.

This was OK with me, as I was through with my work there and I was also through with corporate life once again. I made up my mind I was not going to work for a big company anymore.

I was home for a few days when the phone rang. It was an individual I had met briefly at a meeting. Mike ran a company that did technical writing and illustrating of technical documentation for companies in the area. He was wondering if I'd be interested in helping him with a project he had for one of those companies, Johnson Controls. Mike told me what the pay would be, which was the same as I was earning at my previous job, and that I would work in my own office at home. This was OK with me, so I started immediately. Over the next couple of years, working with Mike, I wrote material for Johnson Controls but also for Runzheimer International, Giddings and Lewis, and others.

My office at home had expanded to include a more powerful computer, a better printer, and Internet service. Things were looking up. Karen had another idea for a book, this was after the L.A. publisher had rejected her first effort. She began working with

Living Then & Now

a friend who knew about setting up a book for printing and publishing and some of the other details of the publishing business, such as cover price and the split between the retailer of a book and a publisher. In the meantime, I kept getting more work through Mike as a technical writer and illustrator. This included writing training materials, which instructors used in their classrooms to teach people how to set up, operate, and maintain equipment, for example, automobile assembly lines.

When Mike left the business, the woman, Janet, who was Mike's contact at the company wanted to know if I could keep working. I said I was interested but Janet called few days later and informed me that the Human Resources department told her that I needed $1 million dollars' worth of liability insurance in order to be one of their vendors. I did not have that but I said I'd look into it.

I called a friend of mine who owned a successful corporation and asked his recommendation. He gave me the name of an insurance agency that specialized in business insurance. I called them and made an appointment to discuss the situation. When I arrived, I told the agent that the company was requiring the $1 million of liability insurance. He thought about it for a minute, and then said, "You don't need that." I asked him why. He replied, "The company's insurance covers you. The only thing you need is insurance to cover anyone who would potentially meet you at your home or office and get injured there." He went on to inquire, "Do you have homeowner's insurance?" I told him we had renter's insurance (we were still living in an apartment at this time). He said, "Then you are covered."

I called Janet the next day and told her what the insurance agent had told me. She said she'd relay that information to the Human Resources department. I never heard another word about needing insurance and remained working with that company for four years.

Eventually the contract come to a close. This was not because of anything I did or anything Janet did. It was because the economy at the time was slowing down and the material I was writing for them was training materials, which, when a company ordered one of their products, was an option. When the economy took a downturn, the first thing to go was options on a purchase contract, like training materials.

After that contract ended, I took on some freelance work, authoring articles for magazines. I also landed a "work for hire" job (no royalties) with a publishing company where I wrote four books in a series about American immigrants for fourth through sixth graders. I also designed and published the initial website for my company, Richard A. Bowen Writing Services.

Then things really changed. With the Internet, suddenly the writing business became a global marketplace. In other words, not only did many more people enter the field with the ability to work virtually from anywhere, but now people with little or no training or education in the field called themselves writers. The logic was if they could put words on paper, they could write. That's how we got product descriptions on Amazon and other sites that are almost unreadable. That's how the field became flooded with so-called writers, many of whom would work for $2 an hour.

As at this time, with the Internet explosion, everyone wanted a website. For the sites, people needed content. I established a contact with a man from California who needed content for several hundred websites. His specialty was developing sites for the various automobile and light truck models, for automotive accessories, for financing a car or truck, for leasing, and for many other aspects of the automotive field. I ended up writing the content for all of his websites. He did not pay very well but I was learning to write for a new area, website content. Eventually he asked me to edit a newsletter he was developing but eventually, he ran out of work.

Living Then & Now

Around this time, I read an advertisement in the newspaper placed by a man who was looking for a writer. I responded and met the man at a coffee shop where he explained his project. He ran a supply chain company in the area but his brother was an investor and financial advisor. He wanted to author a book about his brother, the business he was in, and stories about how his brother helps people. He wanted me to help him write the book and eventually publish it. I accepted and we began work immediately.

We would have a weekly meeting at his office on the phone with the brother, who lived in a different state. The brother would talk about various aspects of the financial advisor/investor field. I was essentially taking dictation and afterwards putting the words on paper. We eventually recorded the phone conversations so I could reference them later, making my work easier and more accurate.

The project was going along smoothly, with me writing up the material, editing it, and the two brothers signing off on it, until one morning when the phone rang. I answered. It was the author's brother. He said, "Stop working on the project. My brother passed away last night." It was a sad ending to the project. I never found out if the book ever was completed or published.

I took on some odd jobs during this time to make ends meet. Also, Karen and I heard about a new online bookstore. It was called Amazon. This company – the same Amazon that eventually became huge – would put our books for sale on their website for free. We jumped on this because it was a new avenue to sell our books. As we were learning the authoring/editing/publishing business, we only had three titles at this point.

After the automotive website work ended, I received a call from a placement service. The gentleman on the line explained that he had found my resume in his files and wondered if I would be interested in a job about 40 miles south of our house in a place called Franksville, Wisconsin. At this point I was tired of the odd job scene and answered in the affirmative.

This was a contract opportunity and when I arrived for the interview, Marcia greeted me. She was in charge of marketing for the company and as we discussed the situation and what she needed, she suddenly exclaimed, "You're a writer!" I assured her I was and that I could accomplish the objectives she laid out. This turned out to mainly be updating "data sheets.," one-page informational publications that explained what a particular product did, how it did it, and which also provided specifications, contact information, and other pertinent data.

This looked like a rather easy job, even though the company had a couple hundred of the data sheets that I would end up updating and re-writing.

Marcia turned out to be a sharp cookie and I enjoyed working with her. Near the beginning of my contract, I had updated a data sheet's information and revised the copy, and I wanted Marcia to read it to make sure we were "on the same page," to make sure I was doing what she needed. I invited her into my office and gave her the sheet I was working on. After a few moments of reading, she turned to me and said, "I have been working here ten years, and never understood what this [product] does. Until now!" I had employed a few tricks of the writing trade to improve the copy, and it obviously worked.

From then on, I spent the next ten months updating their many data sheets. The company eventually asked me to update their instruction manuals, too. When I completed the work and the contract was over, I turned all the files over the Marcia and that was that.

During spare moments while I was working this contract, I was working on a book project I had in mind. Karen had worked with friend on writing and publishing her first book and, as noted, also learned a lot about the publishing business. This prompted me to work on my second book. I wrote the copy, and using some of the layout and design skills I had learned at Snap-on, created a cover. I then laid out the book according to Amazon's specifications, and, ended up self-publishing my third book. I also put

Living Then & Now

my other books on Amazon and also Karen's book. So we now had our own publishing company and four titles and an audio tape (of one of Karen's books) available on Amazon.

A day or so after the data sheet contract ended, I received another phone call. A different recruiter wanted to know if I'd be interested in another contract, this one closer to home. The opportunity was at Johnson Controls in downtown Milwaukee, the company I had previously done some freelance work for through my old contact, Mike. I said I was interested, interviewed, and was soon on my way to a new experience. At Johnson Controls, the company was working on initiating a new process called "document mapping." The idea was to have people, like me and the other three writers they hired to accomplish this task, "map" all of the documentation for their products, in other words assign numbers to the various sections of the document. The objective was to be able to reuse those sections.

The technical acronym for this process is DITA (Darwin Information Typing Architecture) -- technology that helps facilitate authoring, reuse, and translation. Since my time at Johnson Controls, I have often heard about this terminology but, honestly, have not yet run across any company that is successfully using it.

Living Then & Now

The other three writers and I did this mapping work eight hours a day for about eight months. The company also assigned me the job of working with one of their head engineers to write new documentation for some of their products and to update others.

I was learning more and more in my field as the years progressed. My next contract was with a company that created documentation for heavy equipment, such as backhoes and road graders. A person that I met at one of the companies I was working with recommended me. It was part time out of my office at home, paid well, and I worked with another writer and an illustrator to put together this voluminous document that included set-up procedures, operation, and maintenance/service sections.

Of course, I knew little about diesel engines, hydraulics, and the other aspects of these machines, just as I knew little about the other products I had written documentation for in the past. But I learned and most importantly, I learned I did not *need* to know a lot about the products. Research was my best friend but also working with SMEs (subject matter experts) helped me get it right. I could research, write, and illustrate, and I did that to the best of my ability. And then I would have the SME(s) for the project sign off on it. Usually they returned very few markups on the material and I do

Living Then & Now

not recall ever making a huge mistake or providing inaccurate information. Not that I was perfect but by the time I was able to provide a first draft to the SME, I knew the product well and felt confident about where the project was headed.

I next landed a contract with a "supply train" company. This company, which was a division of FedEx, processed recalled and outdated pharmaceuticals from pharmacies, doctors' office, and health care facilities. The company had specific software and had to follow strict, federally-mandated procedures on how it did this, and they hired me to document the software and the procedures. The interesting part here was that the company had a writer on staff but 1) she worked in a different city (Pittsburgh), which made it difficult for her to work on the project, and 2), at this point in her career, she confided in me that she was spending only 10% of her time on documentation and 90% working as a software analyst.

The company had originally developed a software package to run the processing of returns in the plant and in the office, and had modified the package through the years to make it perform the tasks the company required. And a manual existed for that original software; they had simply not updated it. Also, the staff writer had worked on the project and had made numerous notes about the updates, but never verified the procedures with the SMEs.

Living Then & Now

My plan, which frustrated the business analyst (BA) who was tracking my progress and reporting it to management, was to update the manual first, then use it to document the current processes. One potential glitch, in addition to the BA reporting that the process first had to wait until I updated the manual, was that the project required the company to purchase a $900 software package that I needed to accomplish the goal. They did this quickly and I was on my way.

All the SMEs cooperated willingly in providing information for me and even demonstrating their jobs to me so I could document them – except one. This man was so concerned about job security — thinking if I documented his work, he would lose his job to someone else — that he avoided meetings with me and often did not return my calls and emails. I did manage to have a couple of meetings with him but when the contract ended, I regretfully turned over all the material to management with only about 75% of this man's job documented.

While I was at work with the supply train company, my sister told me about a friend of hers who desired to publish a book she wrote. I told my sister to have her friend email me the manuscript and I'd give her my opinion about self-publishing her book. I received the manuscript and read it. This was a historical novel and, I thought, extremely well written. I also thought the story was a page-turner, very engaging. The woman agreed to pay me to edit the material, design a cover, and set up the book for publication on Amazon. The manuscript needed little editing, and setting it up per Amazon specs was relatively easy, as was designing the cover. A couple of months after first reviewing the manuscript, my sister's friend had published her book and she was happy. And I was happy because now I could add another service skills to those that my company offered: assisting authors in publishing their books.

Shortly after the supply chain project ended, I worked on a couple of other interesting ones. This included writing a considerable amount of web content for an attorney's office and working with a realty company. The web content for the law office was all about the various laws, requirements, and penalties in the states of Virginia and Maryland. The content provided information regarding personal injury, product liability, drunk driving, drug dealing, and others. The realty company needed web content for their main website. They operated in my home state of Wisconsin and they wanted content for all 72 counties in the state – what the counties offered in the way of schools, entertainment, recreation, employment, etc.. The idea was to show the attractiveness of each county for those who were considering purchasing a home or condominium in one of those counties. I worked with the law office for six months and with the

Living Then & Now

reality company for almost a year. They overlapped but their deadlines were loose and I had no problem completing all of the assignments they needed.

My next opportunity was with Ashely Furniture Company. This company's headquarters is in Arcadia, a small town in southwest Wisconsin. As a result, many of their workers worked remotely. They needed a writer in the Enterprise Services area for various projects, among them writing on-boarding materials for new hires, newsletter writing and production, and Power Point presentations for their company-wide video network. I did all of these, plus others like designing business cards and writing technical documentation. The contract was remote except for an initial meeting where I travelled to Arcadia to meet some of the Enterprise Services staff. The contract lasted almost one year.

Honestly, every contract I had did not run 100% smoothly. My contract with Ashley required that I attend a 9:00 a.m., Monday morning, remote meeting with the Enterprise Services staff and the head of the department. This was doable but I had a difficult time with the department head on one issue: his method of working with me was to go over each piece that I wrote paragraph-by-paragraph, line-by-line on the phone. My method, which I used countless times with other companies, was to hand over an initial draft and ask the SME to mark it up at his/her/their leisure and give it back to me. Then I'd make the changes, produce another, hopefully final draft, and move on. No matter how I attempted to convince this man to work my way, he wanted it his way. Well, he was in charge, so that's how I worked this one.

Speaking of numerous websites, during this time I also worked with a company based in Los Angeles that produced content for various automotive products and services. Similar to my first web-content project, in addition to car and truck parts, accessories, and financing, this company, produced content for its readers about various automotive repairs and customizing. As a result, I wrote content for repairing wheel bearings, rotating tires, changing oil, tinting windows, replacing head gaskets, installing a new electric window motor -- you name it. I worked with this company twice, once in 2009-2010 and again in 2015-2016.

Soon after, I worked with a couple of other companies that needed web content for their clients. This involved technology, consumer products, how-tos, etc. One of the more interesting and challenging contracts I landed was with a company that produced blogs for business and industry. These included blogs about management strategies and business practices. I found many experts online who provided their opinions, expertise, and experiences that I could draw from to help me provide overviews, techniques, and insights.

Living Then & Now

All of these clients provided references for me to use, links to information, and outlines about the post that they wanted me to follow. These helped the company direct me so the result was what they wanted. This information made my job easier, and while I would check out the information they provided, I would also research my own sources, unless the company was strict in wanting me to use exactly the source they specified. Either way, they got what they needed. I was never late with a deadline nor did the client ever outright reject any of my work. It helped, of course, to ask questions if anything was unclear to me, but these people were professionals, too, and they for the most part provided expert project direction.

My next challenge was writing military specifications for fire retardant equipment. The client was a firm building ships for the U.S. Navy. A former co-worker referred me to a company who needed three writers to complete this project. The project was somewhat mundane and did not require much writing but it paid very well and I did the work from my own office on my own time.

A short while after finishing the military specs project, I received an email from a Minneapolis company that needed a writer for a textbook project. The totally remote project entailed writing a chapter of a technical college textbook about servicing and maintaining heavy equipment. As I found out, it

Living Then & Now

also included providing illustrations, creating a glossary, and writing test questions and answers. I had done something similar in the training materials I had written for Giddings and Lewis and I turned out to be a good fit for this project. After I successfully wrote the first chapter, they assigned me another chapter. Then another and another. I ended up writing seven chapters for them. Great project.

Following this, I had two not-so-great projects. Both involved reviewing consumer products. I had to research the product, make a decision on which one was the best, second-best, third-best, and so on, and then write about the pros and cons of each. The pay was low, the deadlines were tight, and the work was grueling. I did it for the money and when both projects were complete, I realized this was slave labor, and not worth it unless you like slave labor.

Bear in mind that all the while I was assisting authors in publishing their books. As I did previously with my sister's friend, when I received the manuscript, I looked it over to decide whether I could work with the person but also to determine the condition of the manuscript. In other words, was the manuscript in OK shape as far as being well-written enough where I could simply edit it for grammar and construction issues, after which we'd have a publishable document. (If the manuscript was in tough shape, I'd work with the author on that aspect.) I then discussed other areas such as the cover, back cover, and any illustrations the author may want and also the formatting involved and the effort it took to list the book for sale. I'd produce a quote around all of these variables and if the author accepted it, away I went.

Some of these book projects moved along rapidly, especially if the author had a reason to make the book available quickly, like if s/he/they needed it for an upcoming class. In fact, most came together quickly. But others took more time, especially if the author was busy doing other things in their lives or working a lot.

I helped a minister tell her life story with her inspirational, autobiographical piece; I worked with a private investigator who wanted to assist others in becoming their own P.I. through the tips and direction in his book; I worked with a chiropractor who assisted his clients with way more than chiropractic, such as diet, exercise, attitude, etc.; and quite a few others in various walks of life.

I choose to focus on the man who wrote the book about his career as a private investigator for a moment. He had worked with a person who convinced the author that he was a writer and editor and that he could help him publish his book. But the person basically took the money and ran. The author took a chance with me after the previous person burned him, and I was humbled that the

Living Then & Now

author had faith in me, whom he did not know except for some emails and phone conversations, to get the job done, which we did.

During this time I worked with a company that writes software that analyzes other software for security and vulnerability issues. They needed numerous blogs about various aspects of their business and products to help potential buyers of the software understand how the products work, why they needed the product, and how their company might benefit from using it. As with previous contracts, the company was great with supplying me with the information I needed, including references and access to SMEs.

Well, that's about it from my end. My career is ongoing. It has its difficult challenges, and it has its great rewards. One challenge is people with no training or education in the field who masquerade as writers, and who will work cheaply and who end up putting garbage out there to make it difficult for the real writers. A further challenge is AI. It's been my experience that artificial intelligence, while it may help some people create written materials, can in no way replace a person.

I choose not to denigrate people or processes but rather encourage people to find out for themselves by comparison and actual experience.

Wrap-Up

The benefits of my career in writing have been astoundingly wide and varied. I have met and worked with people from all walks of life, from staffers to middle managers to presidents and CEOs of companies. I have worked on projects from writing about dog shampoo to airplane repair to management strategies and everything in between. I have learned to adapt to multiple new technologies, from using an IBM electric typewriter to a MacIntosh computer and software, from paper files to electronic files, from film to digital photography, from interoffice courier to email, from library research to the Internet and Google, and many more. It's been a great ride and it continues. Thanks to all my clients, co-workers, and friends. I'm eternally grateful.

About the Author

Richard A. Bowen has been writing since high school and has authored numerous books, blogs, and articles. He currently lives in Wisconsin with his wife Karen and their pets. Visit his website at www.RichardABowen.com.

www.ingramcontent.com/pod-product-compliance
Lightning Source LLC
Chambersburg PA
CBHW070202230526
45471CB00002B/783